Phantom Camera

Jaswinder Bolina

New Issues Poetry & Prose

A Green Rose Book

New Issues Poetry & Prose
The College of Arts and Sciences
Western Michigan University
Kalamazoo, Michigan 49008

First Edition, 2013.

ISBN: 978-1-936970-13-1 (paperbound)

Library of Congress Cataloging-in-Publication Data:
Bolina, Jaswinder.
The Phantom Camera/Jaswinder Bolina
Library of Congress Control Number: 2012940512

Editor:	William Olsen
Managing Editor:	Kimberly Kolbe
Layout Editor:	Elizabyth A. Hiscox
Assistant Editor:	Traci Brimhall
Art Director:	Chris Fox
Designer:	Ashley Cameron
Production:	Paul Sizer
	The Design Center, Frostic School of Art
	College of Fine Arts
	Western Michigan University
Printing:	McNaughton & Gunn, Inc.

Phantom Camera

Jaswinder Bolina

New Issues

WESTERN MICHIGAN UNIVERSITY

Also by Jaswinder Bolina

Carrier Wave

For Leah Blaise Connor
Naomi Leanna Oberg
Sam Mark Oberg
Zac "Tall" Oberg

Contents

Tidal

For nothing but throwing bottles or bodies into, the ocean is overkill.
I haven't seen an ocean in years, but I know one's out there, poised
like a cassette tape tucked into an answering machine nobody's calling.
I speak low, a foghorn diffusing on ocean, carry home, a barge
carrying on ocean home. I imagine ocean as an undulation,
like traffic or gravity, what appears heavily then recedes again into itself—

There's so much more I could tell you. Maybe you know enough
already and are wary of disclosure. You can't trust anyone anymore
what with poor God dead, but still I reach for you, and you don't answer
for so long, it's as if I'm mimicking the old-fashioned kitsch and flow
of prayer, but still I reach for you and your mute face
as if this might stretch and smooth the crease in my brain
where the self accumulates. I want to tell you I'm guilty of so many things
but these aren't the worst of me. I want to tell you my story is long
and filled with moments of absolute irrelevance, but still I go careening
over summer's muggy surface, under winter's blanket renunciation.
Still I hurtle through the fortnights and small eras of the city,
the Geiger counters about their steady, nuclear clucking,
the air unrelenting so that I and the architecture erode a little each day
in the damp build of weeks till the solstice, and I wake up every morning
in an extraneous light, national light, periscope light of the sun
ricocheting down through tall buildings, and say into the flat planet
of the mirror, *I'm the one sent to replace you.*

Municipal Vistas

The telephone poles lashed and strobed by an electrical storm
in the bus window, we must've been halfway through Uptown
when you clutched at my poncho and said, *Bill,*
are you seeing how this deluge of photons everywhere overwhelms

the tiny cockpit of the eyeball! In this hullabaloo of thunder!
In the damp overthrow of April! You said, *And think*
how the plains crumple into a pageant of hills
at the feet of our mountains and of our noble woods

with their shotgun shoulders and the labyrinthine city in which
our punk-haired rosebushes are a berserk argument between
the trees and hydrants! You said, *Isn't it all such a wingding!*
But I said, *In our chintzy country?* I said. *Here we're insipid,*

eager only for diversions and chic habiliments. I said, *We're daft*
and out-of-proportion, vain and cussing each other in traffic
as if the ego is something other than a pesky infection
of the corpus, as if the corpus isn't downing its espresso

and everything bagel with cream cheese en route to the office park
of nonexistence. It's commuting, at least, out of the palace
of our best efforts! you said. You said, *At least look how bonny*
I am in this skirt the color of a hatchet wound blooming!

You said, *Look how the telephone lines droop and festoon*
all our avenues, how the rain paratroops totally reckless
out of the cloud! See how it has no religion? How nothing
deters it? But I said, *We're more like the gutter spouts*

or drainage grates or the steam rising from asphalt
like end credits after the squall. So you said, *Here's a rope,*
you dolt. Go climb a tree. I knew then I'd deflated you brutishly.
I said, *O, please forgive me!* I said, *Here's a bouquet*

made of moths ruddied by stoplights, o, please forgive me!
Here's the jamboree of a crosswalk, if you'll only forgive me!
I said, *Here's the sound like ovation the rain makes on rooftops,*
won't you forgive me? But you didn't forgive me, cratered

as you were in a rut of futility, so I felt futile too, the steel
cranes unmoving over their worksites, under a serious voltage.
I said, *Ain't this a shame?* You said, *Ain't that the way?*
And we felt more grown-up then than we'd felt before,

more sober and American than we'd ever been before,
motoring along the steep crag of the curbside, a fracture
of rivulets garbling the windows. I said, *Honestly, Amelia,*
what is it all these chipper tourists come photographing?

Mine Is the First Rodeo, Mine Is the Last Accolade

I'm grateful to the man now sleeping with my ex-lover.
It's true I loved her, but it's right that someone be with her now
in the dark hour of our republic. Life is no good anymore.
There are no jobs and no money, so it's good
that someone be with her now under street lamps filtered
through sheer curtains at night, the pale approximation of daylight
illuminating the outer slope of my ex-lover's left thigh
and the asymmetric birthmark located there I thought
resembled the bust of Martin Van Buren,
which that man should smooch now and cherish
as I did those tender hours on the other side of time and the republic
when in the opulence of waking I'd move to the window to squint
at the dapper bodies passing which seemed then to know
where they were going. What awaited
when they arrived there. No job, no money,
I'm grateful for the man now nuzzling and elating with my ex-lover,
how she survives with him this dark hour, its sad redundancies,
the human condition like a phonograph skipping,
which is the condition of urging the same thing over
and anticipating a different result. How dull it is,
its mimeographed disasters, dull how the bankers are
offing themselves now in morning again, leaping from windows again,
the republic fretting as if it's the first republic, the first dark hour,
and dull the way the man drives daily at daybreak away from my ex-lover
in an extravagant light believing that if he does, that when he does,
he'll be the first to hurt her. O enduring sun.

Stump Speech

Street lights swing elliptics in the wind, so shadows
of the nation cast wobbly. I understand how near
you are to the tipping. I understand how the
sensation is of moving very quickly

as if along a high scaffolding where the danger is in
becoming too conscious of the easy, animal rhythms
of walking. You're trying not to over-think it and
you're trying not to not think of it either.

Bacteria in the headwind, free radicals in the cola,
there are double agents in the cannery. You feel
small and you remember the nation. You remember
how you sat once on your porch beside the bracken
patch in front of the house, how the katydids
regaled you.

You remember the reeds as fuzzy exclamation
marks lining the creek, your mother's love, how the
ice cream truck ambled by singing its clumsy,
headless song. You didn't even think of germicide.

When you grew large and employable, the nation
employed you. When you spoke, others feared and
adored you. When you ventured, everywhere there
was fear and adulation. When you were young and
that was the nation.

But lately, the cicada hum sounds for you. A lamppost in vapors stands for you. The tilt-o-whirl is your erratic sense of interior. Lately you think you are nearly no longer the nation.

You hear a constant and tinny noise, the wind is a wall. Lately, the oak trees are entirely emptiness in the way emptiness is heavy and wooden, the nation a hallway all vanishing point no conclusion.

I'd convey you out of the dusky corridor. I'd deliver you into the tree-shaded backyard of good friends you haven't seen in many years. I'd bring peaches and cream and give you a ride to the airport.

I'd do your laundry and offer you a flower or the feeling of someone coming toward you through mist with flowers, the feeling like waking to a warm rain or walking in the damp radiance of sun after rain,

the nation flawless and naked and crooning beside you, its pledge of fidelity, its ripe promise of industry, its squadrons alert on the prairie, its satellites unblinking over every sea.

Panjandrum

Hallo, Dave! David, hallo! I'm having so good a day,
I don't need you and don't need the hulk of you sulking into
my dance hall with mud on your boots. I skip up
the courthouse steps vindicated and free, lift up my robes
and issue exquisite decrees, so no, I don't need you,
your grassroots and counsel. It's too good a day, Dave,
and I don't need you or dour Faisal or any of the grim Ethels,
your protests and woe! The soldiers stomp onward,
and they stomp onward with glee, so no, they don't need you,
Bertha, your washcloths, your pathos and honey. I indulge
extravagantly in legumes and peaches, I pour water
into a wine glass and call this one kind of miracle, I ask
my spleen for nothing, but on it goes with its spleening!
So no, I don't need you, Chester, I don't need you, Marie,
your picketing and screeds. The wan girl standing
on the corner with a clipboard and a bandage on her back
covering a new tattoo is another I don't need.
I don't need to know her name or in which tearoom
she partakes of oolong, making delicate gestures.
Darfur is far away, and Pyongyang is far away,
and the gum-rot, rusted armpit of the city is a glittering
mosaic of broken bottles of Yoo-hoo! and Pabst and is fed
and is sated and free, so she doesn't matter as you don't matter.
Aw, Dave, I'm having too good a day, and I don't need you
and don't need you, and if you should come this way
by buggy, hybrid or electric, or by a wide, purposeful stride,
you'll find my face is the face on the coinage, my voice
is commanding as the ping of a fork striking a crystal decanter,
and I'm presiding under the meniscus of night sky, luminous
and solitary as a firefly beneath a field of stars unconstellated.

Portrait of the Minor Character

In my life as a novel, you're the haberdasher in tweed
closing up shop in October on Oak Street who I nod to

while I stride urgently to meet with urgent others.

Or maybe, my knapsack riding the conveyor,
you're the woman at O'Hare security inviting me

through the metal detector
or the attendant admitting me when I arrive,

breathless at the gate.

You ladle soup into my bowl in the hospital cafeteria.

You're Iowa in the novel about Chicago,

are background radiation, invisible and pouring
out of the perforated night

onto the pier I walk to the edge of.
Or you are the pier.

You're someone I mention in a story
about my industrious past

or you're lounging in the afternoon
of my industrious future

on a boat on the water I wave to,
and though you don't know me, you wave back

because you're the sort who waves to strangers.

In my life as a novel, I hasten and blur

past you on the hotel escalator,
or I shiver out of focus beside you

in the frigid evening of the Argyle Avenue Elevated
on my way to a shindig at Tate's place or Enrique's place,

or I'm flotsam in your proximity in the saloon,
days without eating, days without Suzie.

Or the other idea that you're not in the novel at all

but are somewhere over where you are
where life is like what life is really like

in conversation with others in amusement or in consolation
in the elsewhere of your real life

where you're doing so well and so much without me.

Make Believe

We will eventually be archaeology, but now in America

I tell my young daughter the new headlights are a bluish-white instead
of the murky yellow of my upbringing.

She's busy with her bubble-making, her dig in the flower bed,
her pantomimed banquet, phantom guests

dining on her small handfuls of weeds and grasses.

Precisely, the lit up jackrabbits appear in peculiar blue candor
under the stoplight dusk,

pigeons hued reddish are garrulous and incomprehensible as drunks
at the end of the cocktail hour.

It's that time in America when the air is overgrowth.

The piquancy of coriander neighbors allowed to flower mingles
with fragrances we douse our clothes-lined laundry in each week

to cloister the body's reeking.

Truck smoke from the interstate.

I'm out-of-doors, which is to say nature is hemmed in by doors, which is to say
nature is a category of my making, and I can't say why the skittish,

black bugs flit into the house when there's so much turf afforded them already,
but tonight I'll crush a few with a *Newsweek* before sleeping.

Now, it's that time in America in the out-of-doors beneath tree and trellis

and vapor trails of overnight flights
fare-thee-welling to London and Morocco.

Brandy in soda water, a xylophone jingle of the ice, I sit in my Adirondack

without my minute, Midwestern wife
who Tuesday returns from her summit in Cleveland.

It's that time when I'm alone in America with my young daughter who startles

herself realizing the woodpile beneath that black oak is itself formerly a tree,
and she wants to know whether these trees have feelings.

It's this acquaintance with death she so improves upon annually.

It's in this precise moment in America that I realize this acquainting, this becoming
familiar, this cordiality with death is the entire task of her growing older.

Next year her ficus will die and the next year her minnow will die,
and it's in these moments in America

when my daughter's plump lip quivers in a preface to bawling,
when I'm alone and can do too little, I say,

I'm sorry life is too much, my love, I'm sorry my love, it isn't enough.

Troposphere

Hosanna to the gracious and eminent genius I never heard of.
Hosanna his opera opening in Minsk, his art exhibition in Zurich,
his graceful field theory and double album of great hits.
Collegiate bohemians must tack portraits of him in lucid reverie
to walls over their futons, over secondhand BarcaLoungers
in wisps of incense above the clutter of ashtrays on cardboard boxes
doubling as end tables. Their instructors might pant after
his endorsement and their boyfriends probably swoon,
but I never heard of him. I've read dozens of books
and never once encountered his sequence of fractured sonnets,
never once his instructional manual. I never rode in a Bentley
or wore a TAG Heuer or had his skill for dismantling his critics
so magnanimously, but this theme of not doing, of not achieving
is one I return to often driving past the pale motels that flank
the tollway west of Aurora or when I'm deliberating
between heads of lettuce in the Dominick's grocery store or when
I'm digging into the pouch of peanuts on a shuttle to Annapolis
conceding to myself I never will have cause enough
to purchase a tuxedo, how this is true for most of the lot of us,
most of us fungible bodies thrown at a problem not altogether
certain what the problem is, as in war only less heroic, as in revolution
but less righteous. No confetti or bunting will greet me.
I suppose it's good to arrive at this early, too, so as not to feel
threatened by it at some critical juncture as when attempting
to grease the palm of a maître d' or contest a traffic violation
or when children are watching. No atrium is filled with any experts
awaiting my expert opinion, and it's this sense of feeling finished
with the self I return to most on warm, overcast evenings
in my minor apartment listening to the high-pitched locomotive
of cricket noise, buzz of the high-tension wires, the neighborhood
of intermittent elms, how far away everyone is, and me nearly dozed
on the sofa watching the ball club drop another series to Houston,
the squat shortstop up for a day or two to take the place
of one of the extraordinary wounded before returning to the minors,
to the slow crawl of bus travel across Carolina, to a spot on the bench
in a rainout, slouched and spitting sunflower seeds into a puddle.

My Face Instead of the Virgin Mary

In an oxidation stain beneath the freeway overpass
and in a smudge of oil on the window pane

and in the scorched surface of a slice of toast,
my face instead of the Virgin Mary.

My face in Lourdes and in Clearwater
and in Finca Betania.

The sun is not a rose.

Red helmet of evening,
the sky is not a cornea.

My plain face instead of the Virgin Mary
unable to relieve or to heal you.

The constellation above me
is winking beacons of the radio relay tower.

The constellation beside me is the fizz
in a ginger ale catching some light.

What appears cradled in my arms
is only a loaf of rye.

Why would you tell me the things that hurt you?

Course In General Linguistics

If I'm going to be attacked, let it be by a rare pathogen

not some yokel hurling
sand nigger at me

from a beat-up Cutlass Ciera at seven a.m.

If I'm going to be attacked,
let it be by asteroid or metastasis

not the toothless yahoo of my expectations.

What I can't understand is
who has the energy to be a xenophobe at seven in the morning.

Not me anyway, though I had energy enough
to think of language.

I don't mind being attacked,
but let it be by precision guidance

or satellite track, a line item in the budget

instead of a bland epithet. *Sand nigger,*

he hollered hoping for a rim shot maybe
or maybe meaning, *Go back where you came from!*

How could I explain I had nowhere to go,
no other way to get where I was going,

and I hadn't meant to trouble his morning
and hadn't meant to make him uncomfortable,

but if he thought *he* was uncomfortable,
I mean the guy howled

Sand nigger! at me
and there were people around.

I was so embarrassed for them
looking so uncertainly to me and what I might do,

so I set about explaining
how he'd gotten the country of origin wrong,

how my folks are from green fields
and there isn't any sand there,

and sure I'm brown, but I'm harmless.

I mean, I don't even believe in God.

Then I thought of all the people he meant
when he offered *sand nigger*

and thought of all the people
he might've foisted *sand nigger* upon

that morning even, and how even now
he's probably somewhere in his Cutlass Ciera

shouting, *Sand nigger! Sand nigger!*

at over-baked socialites stepping out of tanning salons,
squinting into the sun,

and how all us *sand niggers* are in this together.

Anyway, he shouted *sand nigger*,
and all the others I told this to all agreed

it was *hideous* that he shouted *that* at me,

so the signifier *hideous* signified *that*

which signified *sand nigger*
which had meant *hideous* all along,

but I could barely blame him,

all that concrete and glass
having fallen out of blue September,

the god-awful, sand-nigger sky,

how it was *his* sky, and I wanted then
to embrace him

and murmur, *I understand,* or, *I'm sorry,*

or, *I want to stab you in the heart,*

meaning, *How easy it is to wound,*
how much easier to be the wounded.

Ultrasonic

Mother, that's my batty consciousness   assembling inside you.

Comprised as it is now of meat and diction,

in the lunar hues of this image,   subaquatic, parasitic,

ungoverned by any syntax,

it's an organ without any function.   It becomes and becomes

until it becomes a thing excreted,

like an utterance,   like a dispatch addressed to no recipient.

In the future it'll drive a big car.

It will amble and brood and canoodle too   in the funny buzz of

afternoons in the beer garden

in an altered state, we say,   as if the mind is performing

an acoustic version of its electric album

or is a foreign lingo in bad translation,   but in this early portrait

the soma poses schematic,

a charcoal sketch of the self,   this inkblot anatomy

without music, without politic,

without ethnic or epistemic,   no language bickers and rambles

in its braincase, no neural parliament

in session in its soft tissue,   this mute floret,

dumb as deity, dumb as moon.

Portrait of the Self

The self wakes up extruded of whimsy. No tango in
its Rorschach, no mermen in its sea. The self with
its ordinary appendages, all radial arm and ulna, no
wing. Solemn face of the self reflected in the black
plastic of the microwave door, the self so somber
nobody would want to hold its hand at a roller rink
any longer than two revolutions. Basket case of the
self with its penchant for gloom. Beneath its
accouterments the self swears it's not so frumpy.
The self insists there are fairer editions of itself:
radiant in a dance hall or expert on a call-in radio
show, executive self on the board of directors,
drunk and fond self so earnest and inconsequential
it's necessarily beautiful. Like a photograph lying in
a field of snow. Fragile beast of the self, hid animal
in a cap and a coat in the damp cold of the solstice.
Turbine of the self exhaling phantasms of steam.
Something escapes it. In death, it wants only to be
itself again. In life, it wants only to conquer itself,
the self in its honest hovel honestly attempting to
void its desire. Self as the pagoda and also the idol
cross-legged and worshipped there. The self with its
mule and its bindle already yearning for so little.
Only the gig in Boca and a bungalow on the shore.
Only vision and dental and the modest attention of a
bashful cadre of devotees. Only to grow tomatoes in
Boca beside a humble but ample veranda. Only this
and then, the self tells itself. Then, it would abstain
from longing. Then, the self would desist, in its hut
of contentment, bronzed and blithe self there on its
porch with a vermouth and a tomato in an early or
an expiring light.

Body in a Phone Booth

The body in the phone booth   is a curious whodunit, is a theatric
in which grotesque death interrupts
and leaves the body in a mute
derangement, the crumpled corpse
caught broadcasting aspersions
or committing a clumsy espionage
now dropped like soiled laundry
in a glass hamper, so the dial tone hums
from the handset, but the body's ear
is switched off, its circuit disconnected,
and somewhere—Johannesburg
maybe or maybe Lima, Peru—
some handler or mistress fidgets
the night anticipating
the startle of a telephone bell.

A body in the phone booth   grants the booth a sense of perpetuity,
the body a temporary occupancy:
You stood provisional
under the permanent sky.
You were out of quarters,
the automatic voice
on the line reiterating,
If you'd like to make a call,
please hang up…
This expelled you then
into frantic morning, your body
moving like a quick tourist
through a perpetual Chicago.
You were a word,
the booth a mouth
you'd been spoken out of.

This body in that phone booth   is a longing for elsewhere,
for rough shrubs at the foot
of a hill in the rock-littered,
lidless night of the desert.

A phone booth is there,
is an adorable carnival
in its small fluorescence
beside a stygian interstate.
You'd step into it.
You'd stand there awhile.
You'd dial a number
you'd never call again.

That body in this phone booth   is a case of specific wanting
wherein I see your body
in a snap-button shirt, a skirt
the color of brushed aluminum,
and want to be in cramped quarters
with you. *My body
in your phone booth*
is the invasive sense
of sex, smothering
and wet, how I impose upon
and inhabit your cordoned
spaces, but *Your body
in my phone booth* is a song
of devotion in which I invite
your intrusions, surrender
the clicker, let you pick your side
of the bed, and concede
the last of the kettle corn.

Our bodies in a phone booth   is a diorama, is our place
in the narrative,
how we stood,
gripping receivers,
and spoke to one another
in glass shanties
the way the ancients

howled from trees
or murmured in mud huts,
set signal fires
and transmitted
their stark messages
in a grammar of smoke.

The body in a phone booth   is the antique metaphysic,
is the cloistered subject
apart from the objects.
In the museum of natural history
Sara says, *Think of the self
like the body in a phone booth*,
so all afternoon I picture
myself in an encasement
circa February 1997, my body
in a plaid flannel shirt,
my mouth almost open,
my slack jacket hanging
like a dead cat from my hand,
I'm about to say something.
I look like an artifact,
precious and defeated.

Portrait of the Village

We believe in God the way the blind must believe in color,
the deaf in rondo. We and the children are abundant and named
after saints and angels. Lailah is dyspeptic, Ezekiel horny,
Helena terrorizes Gabriel with a bullfrog commandeered
from thick muck that borders the river. Our bodies cruise
around in cars the way the mind cruises around in the body,
the streets and boulevards named for famous bays
we haven't sailed to. I own a colonial on Guantanamo Road.
Theresa is a boarder at the women's inn on Bengal.
To witness her arrival weekly at banquets in the village
is a deluge of the sensory, a bottle of Chablis cradled
like a musket in her right arm, her fingernails the hoods
of ten red Edsels, her floral prints, her black Pumas,
her cardigan clearly. I'm her devotee, in love in the village
and with the village, which isn't to say life is so much better here
than elsewhere but that it fits together like a prong in an outlet,
silent and electric, which isn't to say life is so much better here,
but that the horror is a delicate drone in the offing like gears
of an elevator buzzing beneath the Muzak. We understand others
in the elsewhere are lasing gazebos and strafing begonias,
we understand the horror will not end in some bodies
smooching exuberantly, but in the village sodium lights halo
the grain silos, the firmament entwines with girders
of the industrial bridge I'm not leaping from, a propane flame
waves its pale blue banner over the verdant bulge of the landfill,
and my arm parts the lazy pollen of afternoons with Theresa.
All autumn we are unobtrusive as clean laundry left in a basket
in a quiet apartment on a quiet corner of the village
where no-one is waiting. When winter arrives belated,
we walk out into the avenue into a snowfall so thick it's as if
the whole scene's coming in over a faulty antenna.
Our bodies in white noise. The village in a crystalline rainfall.
The snow as one kind of atmosphere falling out of suspension.

Aviary

do you remember the time we didn't go to Topeka
we were ready to go with our sandwiches packed
and you had your harpoon and I had my headdress
but we didn't go though we agreed it totally boffo
we could go to Topeka whenever we liked
but I said I'd rather live here than Topeka where
all they have is a crummy zoo and whoever
heard of Topeka anyway so we didn't go
and spent the day instead alphabetizing
the pantry quipping how this had become *going*
to Topeka we composted our leftovers we purchased
hand sanitizer and accreted a Volvo a toolshed
some throw pillows we pressed 1 for more assistance
we pressed 2 to return to the main menu we assembled
in portraits accessorized the great room trimmed
our azaleas until all of these became *going to Topeka*
and we kidded everyday after how we were going
to Topeka and going to Topeka but we never did
see a prairie dog or a tornado and nobody ever heard
of any of us lying awake in hammocks instead
of going to Topeka or lit up by a television
in the pallid dusk of not going to Topeka
after returning home late in afternoons of not going
to Topeka or to Tallahassee or Sault Ste. Marie
so when I sit now on the stoop at night and watch
seedpods helicopter out of our tree onto the sidewalk
by porch light I wonder what the coral wants
what the arroyo knows I wonder what the desert
swallows and wonder too about the hills of Topeka
the cliffs and canyons of Topeka its auroras
and cyclones arcane canals and minarets
its manta rays in clear clear water supple rubber trees
its yeti and its swans breathing fire how when zephyrs
run like lucent fabric across the spires of Topeka
everybody there touches the flesh in the soft dimple
above the sternum and hums an anthem
in the language of Topeka which we can nearly hear
as if it's barely past the yellow tollbooth
beyond that blunt and glaring truck stop

on the other side of a modest slope where its people
greet each other in the customary manner genial
and offering *We are real and death is not*
or maybe it's *Death is real and we are not*
it depends I propose on whichever is the fairer grace

If I Persisted for Seven Lifetimes, I'd Spend Six of Them with You

but something in me would
desert you

the way I lie
awake and wait for the turbine

of your breathing
to whir steady and deep

until in your sleep
I feel simple again

like myself
and reckless again

outside the road is the apparition
of a bridge deck suspended

by cones of light
from the lampposts

a drone of rotors and axles
semis about

the slow groan
of departure

but our two snifters sit
in the sink

so a prowler come
purloining might picture you

glad and drinking beside me

our toothbrushes dally
and crowd each other daily

in a cup in the bathroom
so he might wonder

at our life as trajectory
pristine and decoded

and on hearing the warp
of a floorboard

the murmur of our bodies
stirring above him

he might think to drop
deftly out of a window

with a few items to sell
or to barter

for airfare and a room
overlooking a square

so he might step out
of that room

onto his balcony
alone in a foreign light

and feel simple again

feel reckless and modern
and himself again

Postcards

You'd love the stories they tell so often in these parts in which the fish monger dies and for weeks his dog doesn't eat until the dog also dies, everybody murmurs, of a broken heart. All the rickshaw men tell that story and young women in bonnets tell that story; it makes me feel so attached—like a ligament—to the whole shebang of human experience, which is so much less complicated here.

———————

No need to wire money, everything's fine, I'm having a wonderful time dawdling for hours on the mall among the noble truckers and pharmacists on Sundays or at the café beside the barracks where the artillery men indulge in spirits and brie.

———————

Somewhere, I found this photograph of the township in black and white in winter at night or this copy of a print of a painting of the township in sunlight refracted through the smog I've come to regard as lovingly as the egrets here regard their river homes, and I thought you might have it for the door of the fridge or for your cubicle wall.

———————

The weather's been so gorgeous, and I feel so awful for the folks who work here through all this gorgeous weather, but they do work and do work hard so they all acquire the same sort of expression indicative of a quiet, native nobility though they wear such funny hats and tend to their rutabaga patches with an almost religious fervor.

———————

Religion's very big here. As are tulips. They say this is suggestive of the something-of-divinity intrinsic to tulips, but they say it in a way impossible to translate, so forgive me, I won't bother.

———————

On the mesa the other day I looked out across the tracts of umber hemmed together by rows of mangled vines and noticed some kids ditching school to neck in the fields that seem so much more lush than those I remember from home, the kids courting each other with such refreshing schmaltz: *I love you. Here is a tulip. Do you love me also?*

———————

It's all this fresh air here, I can feel myself changing, it's all the red mosses and hand-crafted hubcaps and moving walkways I glide down, I can feel myself utterly altered being here which is so unlike being there where everything's so complicated.

———————

I drink an aperitif distilled of wormwood every morning with a breakfast of baked bananas wrapped in palm fronds. I listen to the mayor on the radio make his daily pronouncement regarding crop height and the anticipated rainfall. It hardly ever rains, but when it does, it rains for months straight, so you never need carry an umbrella except for when you must always carry an umbrella. You see how much simpler everything is?

———————

I wish you were here you'd love it. We nap all through Tuesday and eat horsemeat marinated in lime juice and marmalade.

Listen, I have to admit I wouldn't believe any of that hooey about the dog dying of a broken heart either, but they tell me it died at this very highway exit or in this very bath house converted into a dance hall or behind this very epitome of a Gothic cathedral, so I thought you should have this picture of a dog.

———————

Why I even thought of you I don't know, it's so perfect here, though I did think of you and thought I'd send you some piece of my pristine life without dentistry or tax shelter.

———————

And so you'd know that I and everything are really much, much better and life can really be so serene and simple, I wanted to send you this postcard of a tempest on the plateau, of this cut tulip pinned to a young girl's bonnet, of these regal horses en route to so quiet and so noble a butcher.

Federal Scene

I launched my Conestoga unknowing the menace in the marshlands. I ran into an abutment. I mired my shabby white coach. I waded and scampered, crawled and bewildered. I arrived at your embankment and became enamored then with you, your tank tops and conscience. You were the most beguiling stenographer I'd ever met, the way you'd diligently take down the proceedings adding a judicial directive compelling flamenco or a sidebar on the valor of finch song in a nuclear age, an entry in which the lead counsel declares, *Forsooth!* at that moment during the cross when she really should've declared, *Forsooth!* I adored your anatomy. I said I'd like to get gin drunk with you and pass out on the sofa. I said, *Please do permit me.* You did permit me. So I poured a lake around your dock and strung a line for my laundry. I plucked my banjo on a window seat in sun and was content then with you, our pinkies interlocking on walks on the promenade. In the heady seconds in which a breeze would lift your cuff enough to expose an ankle, I wanted my dust mingled with yours forever and forever, etc. I wanted joint checking. And all through the quick and early hours of our daffy affection, the city grew into the city of a calendar's photograph of the city. The pollen blew into a perfect wire-frame model of the wind. I grew unable to distinguish your spirit-fish from my idea-bird. You'd claim you didn't photograph well, and I'd counter, *Darling, my darling, but what photograph could contain you?* and become convinced our municipal banter played a critical part in the federal narrative. I'd blurt, *I feel patriotic on the tollway!* I'd announce, *I feel industrious in the grocery store.* It seemed any strife that blossomed then would falter, the national anxieties quickened then slowed to a saunter, all our coffers swelled, and I'd insist unto morning that these were the first days. I'd say, *These are the first days in the new life,* as if the statement was a gift of rice and morning a broke and wretched country. I'd say, *I am born again in the new life,* but not in that arcane, religious way. I'd declare, *Forget Jesus, I'm amazing in the sack!* I was an enlightened animal. I was a delicate bear. The afternoon tinted honeydew. The afternoon a balm that spread itself over the empire so that departing the breezy loft on Catalpa in afternoon you'd check your reflection in the stainless steel of the toaster, hold the glint of the box with one hand and solve the jigsaw of your hair with the other, and you and I and America would be thinking, *This goes here,* or, *This goes here,* and how certain this seemed, and how certain we seemed.

All My Darlings

I'd even now been thinking of you very deeply. I'd seen a Corvair
rusting on a Tuesday and recalled that summer we spent driving.
I noticed a drawbridge drawn tall and remembered
you drinking a Pete's Wicked arguing the relative merits
of the founding fathers. How you lauded Alexander Hamilton.
How your eyes accounted. Even now, the drunk-seeming sway
of birches evokes you collecting leaves to press between
pages of your dictionary, a you so vaguely you in a top hat
and the sleek sheen of vinyl boots. Now that gloomy metal cross
atop every steeple in town makes me think of you
thinking of the birds as crossing through a crosshairs.
You were a woman of so elegant a candor. You were a man
of such good measure. Blue was the light of your hi-fi display.
Green, the distortion of your tv screen. Soft, the dilly-dally
of your hairdo. I contain you now the way the ringing ear retains
the thunderclap. Do you still eat three cuts of meat on marble rye?
Do you still get rowdy on Arbor Day and tear down the corridor
scattering your dossier all over so no-one can know you
or tell you apart? No-one can know you or tell you apart. Even now,
all the ratty hipsters become you, and all the blonde diplomats
become you, a you with domestic accouterments, a you with parcels
on the El train gliding through a vapid fog. You who merengue
without me, who see me when I don't see you among the dithering
crowd on the parade ground in your new pair of shoes.

Zirconia

After you wrecked my Chevelle and ran over my dachshund, after you bedded my chiropodist and confessed to the shaman you adored me no longer, after you emigrated to the low country to take up a new tongue and adopt a tropic demeanor, I yearned for one final letter, for a formal armistice or any kind of treaty. But you preferred the rigmarole unsettled. You favored the unended as in the story in which the kid goes lost in the woods for seventeen rainy seasons, for so long he becomes convinced of no salvation and convinced he'll have to live this way, filthy and rootless ever after. Even when he's grown and rescued and returned to the village, to grammar and vaccinations. Even in his grocer's freezer. Even at the Labor Day parade or when he nods off in a recliner or bites into an apricot or feels the first fluttering thrombosis of I-love-you-I-know-not-why, he believes he's a wolf, naked and homesick, feral and wanting.

We Were Blundering Around in the Darkness

It's mere happenstance that I happened to be here, Trudy,
and though I behave as if nothing untoward will happen,
I covet you the way the president-elect must covet time
for exercise and fishing. Still, my intentions are honorable,
my air intending to be incidental as if I were a fieldworker
who deals with real problems for whom paperwork
is incidental, like a catch of dolphins is incidental in the pursuit
of tuna, incidental as the arbitrary execution of a man
innocent of any fraud who hasn't ever conned anything
bigger than a Boston whaler or engaged in any conspiracy
to destroy the government and pervert the course of justice.
He resided quietly on a street quite innocent of bookstores,
and I'm as innocent as he was. I'm a sweet little cat, Trudy,
though it's true I conned him into giving me your home
phone number so I might invite you to take in with me highlights
of the pumpkin festival. Admittedly, the location is entirely
accidental and contributes nothing to the tension between
characters in this poem, but I thought such time together
might conclude with a good deal of kissing, a slurpy smooch
on the ear, and more congratulations before we parted company
with every party in a buoyant mood, so much so it might
become clear to you that my two great loves are tobacco
and whiskey but also you, Trudy, how you find it so difficult
to accept my adulation the way many French leaders
can't accept American dominance. To them, we must seem
the unnatural monsters of fable, crass as the assumptions men make
about women, and their main problem is plain exhaustion
with our youthful enthusiasm, which is plain stupid,
as I'm made stupid, Trudy, captivated as I am by your charm,
and didn't you know that *charm* can refer to one of six flavors
of quark and *quark* can mean a type of low-fat curd cheese
and not at all any sublime, subatomic particle postulated
as a building block of the hadrons which haven't ever been
directly observed but have been confirmed experimentally,
and isn't that idea less convincing than my basest instincts,
my greed and tenderness, my hunger, Trudy,
for you, my panting desire?

Schrödinger's Cat Variation

if she calls tell her the tan blanket in sun splayed on the sofa

is not her torso in repose

if she calls tell her beyond the radiant bulge of the evening star

are pulsars of the flipside

if she calls tell her I'm awaiting the return of her laundry

delicates returned from an indelicate absence

a broken bottle is ground for months on the sidewalk into sand in The Age of If-She-
Calls

I might find resolution if she calls

the horizon in crisp air

the variable at the end of the equation exposed and comprehensible

if she calls tell her I'm maintaining my disastrous momentum

the sun appears and disappears rapidly so shadows hit the ground intermittently

like feet in a tantrum

I won't have anything to do with her if she calls

if she calls tell her she's the cat in the box

and I am the box

tell her I'm having my portrait taken in wind to give the impression I'm moving very
quickly

I'm not running toward the airport

but I'm willing to provide her with posies if she calls

tell her I'm the wolf approaching the boy and she is the boy and I won't believe her if
she calls

but I'm willing to give her the smashed up sandwich I was saving for dinner

I live in Ifshecalls Arizona
                    it is not the saddest place on earth
                                        but the weather is awful

                                                is struck lightning
                            or thunder without any lightning
unchanging
        like a cicada nailed to a tree

                if she calls if she telegrams if she dispatches a pigeon with a message

if she calls tell her I'm awaiting no signal out of the ether
                                        no body in the phone booth

no two tin cans and no taut string between them

Sunday, Sunday

I worried I'd be discovered exactly where you'd left me,
so I leapt up! and drove straightaway to the coastal
metropolis of Sunday in the desert province of Sunday
where everything was just getting started.
The buzzards hadn't even been unwrapped nor the agaves
unfurled nor the nostalgia-making slant of shadows activated.
The haze along the shore infused with a noontime light
to cast the happenings in the matte finish of a studio print.
I felt young and new and the center of attention, and I wished
you could see me there driving my agape convertible
in sneakers and a gingham shirt, slim-fit indigo denim,
and I wasn't smoking a cigarette, but I looked so quintessential
in my dinner jacket that I had the lithesome air of a debutante
drawing from the long white stem of a Pall Mall 100,
so the citizenry all said, *Look how dapper he looks*
driving the diaphanous skyway, look how handsome
he is in the gleaming cavalcade of traffic, how defiantly
he speeds alone in the carpool lane, how elegantly he collects
his many moving violations. You'd settled into a smart apartment
alone with your cat in the capital of the great state of Thursday
with its daunting mountains and bitterroots, the blackened
trunks of its forest in snow looking frigid as a barcode,
but I wanted to glut your inbox then with status updates.
I wanted to text you my brightening outlook in hopes
you'd forget all the troubles we'd run into in the gridded City
of Wednesday where the automatic windows of my rental car
wouldn't roll up in a downpour and my debit card demagnetized
and I showed up so late so often and disheveled we missed
every night of the opera, but I hoped you might forgive all that
and fall in love anyway with the contemporary sense of me,
the Sunday, Sunday, me now appearing like a bleached crane
strutting in shallow marsh water, like an echo in reverse
gradually deafening, like the speck in your radiograph,
the furious whitecap on your sudden horizon, the dazzle
of a satellite fireballing out of its improbable orbit.

Apologia Matilde

I made thirty-seven false statements before the barrister, Matilde.
I was a trite trombonist who shouldn't have been entrusted

with a sublime and delicate melody, Matilde. I hung, for instance,
a left at the White Hen Pantry when I should've gone right.

I stranded the bishop and too early brought out my queen.
It's true I twice voted for Nader.

I abandoned you, Matilde, on the trolley to Milwaukee.

I said the six things aloud I should've left
mute as fog, I thrice broke your heart.

I'm an agent of error, Matilde, of slips and of blunders.

Even so, that black fraction of a grackle left in the thruway
is not the catastrophe I made manifest,

is not the earnest memento of my broke affection on asphalt,
or my token of poignancy.

Those mopey willows don't mope for me, Matilde,
this tattered country isn't my diorama,

though it's true nothing here is quite so correct as it ought to be.

The sun in morning is more white than yellow
as if the sun of some alien planet's alien-wild elliptic,

every interior is an absence, Matilde, in the architecture,
and when I arrive at the arboretum without you,

the oak trees are so denuded, I don't have nerve enough
for a saunter through the barren hour.

There are the several months I spend each day recanting, Matilde.

There are the dopey spiders in the box spring, the ceiling fan whining
nightly, and the droopy fern in the corner there

you gave to me, Matilde, I go on neglecting. I apologize for this

and for everything, for how I wrecked
your September and torpedoed your May, for how I ruined

three weeks in August and made ten mistakes, Matilde,
how exactly eight of them were accidental.

I'm sorry for this and for everything, for the clangor of the tollway
when you are driving, the brutish heat of the borough

where you roil unsleeping, for your turbulent landing
and the chill of the boulevard when you await your tardy ride.

I'm sorry there will be days unlike these in their misery and ardor,

that there will be the optimism of summer after
seventeen weeks of sleet and rain, and I'll inhale the posh scent

of ragweed and think of you, Matilde, tossing your ragged coat
onto a bedpost in a seven-story walkup

or I'll see a ragged coat and think of you in a seven-story walkup exhaling.

I'm sorry the frayed and patched object is imbued with the subject,
and the flawed subject is an aggregate of all its scuffed, precious objects.

I'm the scruffy brown mascot of indefensible things.

I'm sorry you still think of me, Matilde, but me like a composite sketch
based on uncertain eyewitness testimony.

I'm sorry I wronged you so deftly

and sorry the impartial platelets go on clotting,
oblivious tissue goes on healing,

that the reticent stars still deliver themselves one photon at a time,
comets near in oblong, unhurried approaches,

and sorry still, Matilde, that I'm not alone
at the mercy of the gorgeous and lethal aurora,

and I'm not the tallest tower, Matilde, beneath the pink and blind lightning.

Portrait of the Horse

Sometimes the horse is simply a horse.

      Sometimes the horse is a stalwart
      bearer of bodies.

            Sometimes the horse is stubborn,
            refusing to ford the river,

or the horse is a mistake

      in the vapor, what looks like a horse

            emerging out of a thrust
            of fog on Telegraph Avenue.

There's the perpetual feeling of being

      overdressed for summer
      and underdressed for spring.

            I'm variously sweat or shudder.

I mistake the strange bodies
for those I owe apologies to,

      oversleep and open my eyes on
      the clock radio, the time a typo,

            the apartment a disaster.

Sometimes the horse is disaster
or the horse is time in a trot or a canter.

      Sometimes the horse is a boy
      growing in time into a man

            who often laments,
            A horse, a horse, my kingdom, etc.

But there is no horse.

There are two days good and one day bad

without any hint of a horse.

Sometimes speaking about the horse
is a means of avoiding speaking

about myself which is lousy.

Late last night myself
regarding another carelessly.

Late last night my body
with a temporary body.

The horse is the taut metaphor for sex,

but sometimes the horse is the taut silence after.

Sometimes the horse is the silence
after her body rises

in the embarrassment of morning
and leaves,

and this silence is filled
with less than remorse

but with more than indifference.

This is a feeling there is no word for.

What I decided in place of what I needed.

I should eat better.

I should vacuum more often.

I should settle down
and raise a young horse.

Sometimes the horse is unspoken,

the horse is this feeling
that will be forgotten,

is the self unable to alter its ineffable horse.

Late last night, a pervasive clopping
of the horse on the hill.

Late last night, the horse as a foghorn
over the Bay.

I should be rained on.
I should not be forgiven.

Other Anthems

It would be better to lift dumbbells and swim laps,
to make interest payments, clean out the lint trap
and shovel dungarees and linens into the dryer,
but in my weekly tizzy over God and self and country,

my umbrella is hyperextended in updrafts,
my moving walkway is ending, I'm almost unable
to sit quietly reading *Scientific American* in the prim
silence of the Elevated, its stuffy hush, decent

as tan slacks or a fern or the blank surface
of plain water, punctuated solely by the toddler
across the train car screeching in the realtor's arms
who goes on murmuring to her from a copy of *Tortilla Flat*.

In his canny memoir, I'd scarcely register as a factor
of backdrop, and it's better I not begrudge him
his fortitude, how he won't be distracted
reading Steinbeck to a toddler at rush hour,

better I don't disdain his RE/MAX jacket as an emblem
of haplessness or endorse the girl as an icon of resistance,
the quandary of pathos, her florid and reckless yelping
against the placid disaster of this of all possible worlds.

It's better not to wallow so metaphysic and dismal,
better not consider these two a gauzy portrait
of urban dignity, the human ape enduring the modern,
better not ask what the girl wants her father hasn't wanted

more frantically and for longer, better the steady purl
of wheel on track not tangle harmonic with the father's cooing
and the daughter's harsh rebuttal into the fraught chord
this world makes insisting is best, is best, is best.

Oops Canary

Canary, why do you berate me with your idiot warble?

What truth is there in your story?
I know Pythagoras. I know Punnett squares.

I know whales were exiled from the air,

so their mournful, Byzantine songs resound now
over the drab Appalachia of ocean bottom.

Not me, canary.

I'm brown-skinned and slender,
of unremarkable height and blue-collar origin.

I was born in Chicago in 1978.

No brash plumage.
No quench-my-breath-undersea-for-hours.

I was afforded broad tutelage in the liberal arts and sciences,
but none of these is enough to temper the onslaught of winter.

I never really believed they would be,
but I wanted to say *the onslaught of winter* out loud.

When I told you that thing about whales, I was fibbing,
which is also a kind of song.

I only meant to impress you.

Canary, forgive me.
What more to sing is there than that?

Practicum

no theory in my bellyache no theory in the parking citation
no theory in a keen thorn come slicing my animal shin
no Wittgenstein in my carburetor no Heidegger in our foreplay
no theorists in the hot dog stand or theory to refurbish
the famished I want a hot dog not theory I want the heft
of alms not the tear-jerk of the homily no theory to console
the fervent as when I'm fervent blathering and fearful
the beloved will think me a lunatic for proffering illuminated
parchments whole bales of cotton candy every ruble in Eurasia
what I want is to give what's nearly not possible to give
what I want is to not demand so much more for myself
as when too eagerly I adorn the beloved in extravagant kaftans
of such intricate grandeur no body could inhabit them still
I adore the facile logic of the infatuated to the tortured
ruminations of the jilted I prefer our anatomies mingled
in the sweat-making apparatus of the heat wave to the self
fraught and pensive in bleak abstractions of a cold front in April
when the whole city is yearning for the shriek of bluebells
which will in theory bloom though no theory is there
in the pang of our longing for instance when a body longs for
a medic no theory in the concussions that body's cussing makes
as no theory in the obscenity of the wire reports of April
in Tripoli in Dara'a mortar rounds are practice not theory
as in no theory in what the orphan sees when she's being orphaned
people shriek not bluebells not the banshees of theory who would
abstract and decipher this world its caution tape and shards
in hopes of mending it for which I also adore theory
how it wants to give what's almost not possible to give
one day it might schematize the function of our suffering
one day it might answer our eschatology and one day render
a unified field between a theory of the self and the theory
of the Other but today we can ride out early with wineskins
slung over our shoulders today we can drink sangria in the desert
in its exorbitant ruin and you might kiss me hard on the mouth

Portrait of the Memory

in an Oldsmobile   in   thick   boots   bearing   a   gift   of   papaya
          in what resembles an Oldsmobile   w h a t   r e s e m b l e s   a
papaya   the last of January   three   versions   of   ice   on   the
electric lines and elms   the memory stepping   out   of   a
green or a brown car   out of a Buick in   r o u g h   b o o t s
          bringing home a papaya   or a gladiola   or
macaroons   the memory bringing home   its   factory
scent of lubricant   and steel shavings in a Ford   the   memory
home   from   its   shift   machining   hydraulic   cylinders   on   the   factory
floor   the memory home   in   its   scarf   with   macaroons
          or in its parka   which   was   the   color   of   a   papaya
maybe   or maybe July   the humid memory   m a y b e
the memory not bringing   any   more   than   itself   in
shirtsleeves   the   too-warm   memory   in   a   Cutlass   arriving
without any gift at all

This Room, with Arsonist

If you believe in the soul,   you're the thing inside the other thing,

half corpus, half ethereal light,   the idea the body's only necessary
so the soul can inhabit the world.

                                        If you don't believe in the soul,
inside you is a scratchy racket,   a ghastly sizzle and rotor hum,   the idea of the body
as faulty machinery.

Tom says his mother's body couldn't sustain the idea of itself.

                              The inside of an idea is axons rapping dendrites.

                              Inside, everything is verging on rupture.

Inside my blue shirt is the undershirt with a tear in the shoulder,   inside the tear,

the skin inside which is a network of capillaries   blooming when the shoulder catches
an exposed nail in the hall.

Even so, we want to sit and sip our mojitos in sun.

                              In the muggy run of summer,

our faces irradiated   until the skin flakes.

Inside my face is another face come to take its place. It too is my face.

It'll never grace the cover of *Vanity Fair*.
                       It will not be inaugurated.

And this inside the already immense and expanding catalogue of things I'll never
     eventually do.

                    No go spelunking. No passing calculus.
No sub-orbital space flight or cocktails on the Queen Mary.

        Inside the membrane of what-won't-happen-again
are organelles of the what-happened-before.

           Inside, Tom says, is the image of his mother's face,

                                    luminous and holographic in xenon

              beams of approaching headlamps

      or luminous and holographic strolling in sun

but not a lucid sense of what she looked like.

                        The lucid sense of the pier,

the roiling murk of the lake.

Inside the lake are ions in undulation,   and inside *undulation*, phonemes meaning

      a thing billowing with gravity
                  which is invisible but pervasive inside everything.

Tom says after his mother's body undulated with cancer,

it smoldered in the crematory

until all that was left was the idea of his mother's body.
No more strolling

but for these axons and dendrites inside Tom,

the memory as a room with an arsonist inside it,

her face in dissipation,

as inside the match head,   the bright idea of fire,

and inside the flame,   the dark idea of luminosity

as a thing consuming itself.

Elegy

In sun the sunburned skin sloughs off the sunburned shoulder.
Most folks believe this is the body's slow mend.

Most folks believe in the good yolk of the soul.

I believe in autopsy lingo *of natural causes* should be replaced
with *of long-term exposure to the dim, unwavering radiation of the morning star.*

The evening they burn your body,
I step into the garden and arrange a crooked line of birdbaths to skip stones across

until a bell tower tolls its eight arguments against daylight
and the skyline illuminates, ragged and unmended

like a poem turned on its side.

The evening they burn your body,
I believe I'll step into the living room and be greeted by you

or by someone who could play you in a movie.

The curtains are an aurora of earthly proportion.
You don't exist.

A flash igniting the paned glass is the silent lightning outrunning its noise.
You're on fire.

In Another Version of the Afterlife

I regret some of the aftermath but none of the choices I made
during my tenure among the living, which must be
what the villain feels after being villainous,
the adulteress and war criminal also;
matadors and pornographers must feel this too laid up at night,
groggy and unsleeping in ornate haciendas,
but in this version of the afterlife, we don't bother with absolution,
and I come to understand remorse is a byproduct of causality
which is an error of consciousness which is a glitch in perception,
and anyway we're no longer conscious,
not in any way the living might imagine,
so I don't miss much of living: neither bourbon nor orchards
nor season finales, not Venice or syntax and rain,
not sitting in bed eating some grapes with you
in the imperfect darkness of a city apartment.
I forget all this and forget all this until the self is no longer
like a dingbat alarm clock droning all day
from an open window on the other side of a wide courtyard,
its tinny heartache caught in the perpetual cacophony of waking.
Anyway, there are better things to attend to than waking and the self
in the quaint and cobbled Kentucky of the dead
where we don't produce anything of much utility
and we weather the years without slumber and manage for ages
without water and all wear identical blazers and scarves and faces
and everybody answers to the same name,
so one will tip a hat and ask, *Roberta, how is it?*
and another will snap a suspender and reply, *Fine, Roberta. Just fine.*

How to Order a Sandwich

You'll need to climb down from your tree.

You'll have to
stand upright in the tall grass

and wander the savannah
on two feet under nebulae

you can't begin to ponder.

You ought to hoot
and point then point

and hoot until this is language.

You'll learn to coax
the words into whispering

which will permit the inception
of the beloved.

You should crush petals with a stick

and draw bison on the cave wall to
woo her.

You'll leave a handprint.

You'll need to supervise
the advent of seafaring

and oversee the tribe while it meanders

the finicky coast.

You'll learn to bury the corpses.
You'll burn the bodies.

You'll float the dead out to sea.

Eventually, you'll tie a rag to a pole
and stick it in turf

so that you have property.

Plant seeds.
Offer stuck sheep and chanting to evoke   the damp magic of the monsoon.

You'll need to concoct

the arrowhead and sleep
in shifts to guard your compact republic.   You'll stare into embers
of the sentry fire.

You'll inadvertently invent ontology.

You'll think to write your story down
or paint your portrait   and paint the lines parallel,
the perspective atmospheric

until the depiction becomes
a better version of the world.

Even this will be less than you wanted.   You'll weaponize the horses
and mechanize production.

You'll locomotive.

You'll need to be on the right side of any genocide.

You'll wonder why the mind keeps
reaching for meaning

when meaning is
so unaccommodating
to the mind.

You should go nuclear.

You should wrangle genomics
and credit-default swap.

Fashion transistors

and court above your station.
Get a place in Logan Square.

You'll want in-unit laundry
and a brick interior.

You'll want a deli on the corner

and a deli guy who knows your face,
your height, weight, and social security number,

your mother's maiden name

and the names of the boys
to the left of you

in the photograph
of an extinct afternoon

in Wisconsin you keep in a tin in the cupboard
of an un-trafficked hallway.

You'll stand in a slow queue
in the part of August

when the neighborhood is bronzed skin and breezy dresses.

You'll huff your lonely huff

awaiting your turn at the counter.

You should order the grilled chicken
on herbed focaccia.

You should ask for an extra slice
of mozzarella

and a side of aioli.

You'll have to convince yourself you deserve this much.

You'll need to believe
you're owed more than the dead.

The Reluctant Senator to His Provincial Mistress

A sudden plummet startles me out of sleep
in morning, my love, I wake up in the swamp
heat of the District with a numbness in my teeth
not wanting to brood anymore over bankers
bankrupting the commonwealth,
the requisite war and wild tenements,
threats in the weather and activists strewing
their crass grammars on the national mall.
I want to forget the country completely,
its inequity and angst, how it doesn't
seem to recognize the humdrum scope
of its desire. How it believes it'll linger
this way into the next epoch and the epoch after
so that though it thinks of death,
it conjures a death exactly like life
but more temperate, with fewer fatty acids,
our dead pets and relatives resurrected.
I don't believe death will be anything
like America. Mornings, I want, my love,
to abdicate my office for the periphery,
my small life at night on the municipal square,
the dot-matrix clouds scrolling faint and orange
out of an ink-jet horizon, rain a cold pulp
falling on poplars and the infrastructure,
my guilty constituency with you in the coming
haunt of winter when our fountains run empty,
so we hear coyotes in the outskirts wail
at their quarry, the screeching apocalypse
of the rabbit, the hush that follows and humbles
the town. Mornings, I want that quiet to come,
for that silence, my darling, to entomb me.

The Last National

No-one to offer lilacs to, none to sound reveille, nobody to name
and no other to do the naming, to call it *October* or utter *chthonic*
in the last of your language, in your olive and old coat, alone
on the range, you fret your arrhythmias and dyspepsias, your throbbing
Manassas and swollen Tuscaloosa, your early tulips tormented
by a belated Noreaster, all your Mississippis draining into the sea,
the parking meters stopped clicking their strict minutes,
but evening materializes still like Kodachrome does in a chemical bath,
night tectonic and glacial, the fortnights unrelenting and rapid,
you think of your spent lovers, their bodies fluorescing
in illuminated precincts, in foreign apartments, how they're naked there
eating mangos and reading Rousseau and need you no longer,
how you're far from the nurturing heart of the tribe,
unable to ring the hours back in their bell or pour the torrent
back in its cloud, unable to reel the errors back to your mouth,
your Buick abandoned in long-term parking, your split-level ranch
a ruin some schoolgirl might grin a hokey grin in front of
in a bright photograph of ruin, in another dead Memphis,
in that abundant future in which she studies your wrecked stadia,
your landfill and essential graffiti, your curious reverence
for neckties and wrought iron and headstones, your blundering
physics, the cute ingenuity of the I-beam and the Snickers bar,
which her people have no word for, the really big God
they don't believe in, how you thought you were singular,
that no-one could know you, but look how capably she clears the earth
from your eye socket, look how gingerly she excavates your clavicle,
look how her hands pillow your jawbone, this little one, your tiny usurper.

Dénouement

no rogue airliner's sinister trajectory descending   or mushroom of vapor
                                                                 balloooning over the capital

    not the rifle in fury
    seized from its station above the mantel

                        no up goes the ozone
                        down comes the glacier

    no seismic rupture   the rifle already unloaded

not a breathless embrace in a dim garage
while evading the invading army

                        merely the lovers lying asunder
                        in the sudden certain post-coital disinterest

              the dwindling instead of the impending downpour

    the mourners going through the motion
    of exiting wearily out of the crematory

              their catastrophe ending
                                  the continental drift

rain tapering a one-trick pony
all plummet no rise

                        the drawbridges lowered
                        instead of rising toward dull heaven

                        a fat finch settles
            rotund little comma in the rambling statement of the bough

dust motes mingle in the daylight
wingbeats and the discarded

                        the way life ends the way life doesn't

Phantom Camera

Whatever happens here happens for a reason. It so happens
it's not a very good reason. A tactless thermodynamic,
a static interference, the chemical flukes and chance fractures,
but the quality of the light is Algiers by evening,
is Andalusia at dusk. Triggering fireflies are manic
synapses of the garden, a faraway traffic the soft rush
a vinyl record makes, and here you are with your handful
of blueberries and your breezy magazine, nearing
an almost balmy calm, feeling nearly epic and instrumental
when a prairie gust makes a tambourine of the wind chime
tugging it into an abrupt puddle of pick-up sticks
on the patio brick. You take this as a jangly reminder
of what differs between what you're awaiting
and what lumbers towards you with a bludgeon in tow.
What slow artillery launched out of earshot is arced
and nearing, what patient misfortune of cracked glass
anticipates your bare foot on a beach dune next summer,
influenza on a handrail, what lymphomas percolate,
and who will you cuckold and who rat out,
and whose body is that gliding through an eventual ICU
so serenely you'd almost believe it reposed as you are
tonight on your chaise lawn chair if it weren't for
the neurons in you whose single task is disbelief.
But you leave these switched off in the momentary
Barcelona, the dwindling Tunis of nightfall. You kindle
instead that other axon whose errand it is to reassemble
the memory of a notepad you left in the seat-back pocket
of an airliner that's probably ferried it with all your scrawled
remembrances by now to the other side of the sea
so somebody there might discover it. Somebody might
translate and construe. Someone you can almost picture
reading in a remote morning, in whiffs of heather
and guava, and though you're mostly obscured
in the ho-hum arrival of another domestic night,
you go ahead and grin anyway for that other in the indefinite
offing who you can almost make out, who even now
pictures you too, fanciful mammal, you charmed conspiracy
of nucleotides, all your unwitting electrons in their right place.

Notes

"We Were Blundering Around in the Darkness" is comprised exclusively of word usage examples and definitions—or slight variations thereof—found in the *Oxford American Dictionary* for Mac OS 10.6.

Acknowledgments

Grateful acknowledgment to editors of the following journals in which versions of these poems appeared in earlier drafts:

751 magazine	"Portrait of the Memory"
	"Zirconia"
AGNI Online	"Course in General Linguistics"
Anti–	"Municipal Vistas"
American Poetry Review	"Elegy"
	"Tidal" under the title "One Day, Androids Will Have Pudgy Arms and Hug Us Like Mother, but Still I'd Reach for You, Dear Reader, which Is Why I Have So Much Faith in Us as a People"
Best American Poetry 2011	"Mine Is the First Rodeo, Mine Is the Last Accolade"
Black Warrior Review	"Mine Is the First Rodeo, Mine Is the Last Accolade"
BOMBlog	"Practicum"
Cavalier	"Portrait of the Horse"
	"Portrait of the Village"
	"Schrödinger's Cat Variation"
Cincinnati Review	"Stump Speech"
Columbia Poetry Review	"If I Persisted for Seven Lifetimes, I'd Spend Six of Them with You"
	"Body in a Phone Booth"
Ecotone	"In Another Version of the Afterlife"
	"Phantom Camera"
Explosion-Proof	"Other Anthems"
	"The Last National"
	"Federal Scene"
	"The Reluctant Senator to His Provincial Mistress"

Jet Fuel Review	"All My Darlings"
	"Panjandrum" under the title "In My Bright Autocracy"
The Laurel Review	"My Face Instead of the Virgin Mary"
	"Postcards" under the title "Postcard"
Mandala Journal	"We Were Blundering Around in the Darkness"
	"How to Order a Sandwich"
The Missouri Review Online	"Portrait of the Self"
The Offending Adam	"Aviary"
	"Sunday, Sunday"
	"Oops Canary"
Ploughshares	"Make Believe"
Qualm	"Ultrasonic"
	"This Room, with Arsonist"
	"Troposphere"
Quarter After Eight	"Apologia Matilde"
Third Coast	"Portrait of the Minor Character"

photo by John P. Sullivan

Jaswinder Bolina is the author of *Carrier Wave*, winner of the 2006 Colorado Prize for Poetry. His work has appeared in *Black Warrior Review*, *Columbia Poetry Review*, *The Offending Adam*, and in the *Best American Poetry 2011*. He currently teaches at Lesley University in Cambridge, MA.

The Green Rose Prize

2012:   Jaswinder Bolina
Phantom Camera

2011:   Corey Marks
The Radio Tree

2010:   Seth Abramson
Northerners

2009:   Malinda Markham
Having Cut the Sparrow's Heart

2008:   Patty Seyburn
Hilarity

2007:   Jon Pineda
The Translator's Diary

2006:   Noah Eli Gordon
A Fiddle Pulled from the Throat of a Sparrow

2005:   Joan Houlihan
The Mending Worm

2004:   Hugh Seidman
Somebody Stand Up and Sing

2003:   Christine Hume   Gretchen Mattox
Alaskaphrenia   *Buddha Box*

2002:   Christopher Bursk
Ovid at Fifteen

2001:   Ruth Ellen Kocher
When the Moon Knows You're Wandering

2000:   Martha Rhodes
Perfect Disappearance